KNOW-IT-ALL GUIDES

FREAKY FOOTBALL

If being a writer wasn't Nigel Crowle's full-time job,
he'd still be doing it for fun. He's written for
children's TV series like *Tweenies*, *The Chuckle
Brothers* and *Balamory*, and for big stars like
Ant and Dec, Elton John, Lenny Henry,
Caroline Quentin, Donny Osmond,
Basil Brush and Jonathan Ross.
He lives in Cardiff with his wife, son and
dog where his scripts, plays and books
hopefully keep his family:
(a) occupied
(b) amused
(c) in the manner to which they've
become accustomed (especially Dexter Dog.)

D0526267

Know-it-All Guides by Nigel Crowle

CONQUERING ROMANS
FREAKY FOOTBALL
INCREDIBLE CREATURES

KNOW-IT-ALL GUIDES

FREAKY FOOTBALL FAR-OUT FACTS to impress your FRIENDS!

Nigel Crowle

Illustrated by Martin Chatterton

PUFFIN BOOKS

Published by the Penguin Group
Penguin Books Ltd, 80 Strand, London WC2R 0RL, England
Penguin Group (USA) Inc., 375 Hudson Street, New York, New York 10014, USA
Penguin Group (Canada), 90 Eglinton Avenue East, Suite 700, Toronto, Ontario,
Canada M4P 2Y3
(a division of Pearson Penguin Canada Inc.)
Penguin Ireland, 25 St Stephen's Green, Dublin 2, Ireland
(a division of Penguin Books Ltd)
Penguin Group (Australia), 250 Camberwell Road, Camberwell, Victoria 3124,
Australia
(a division of Pearson Australia Group Pty Ltd)
Penguin Books India Pvt Ltd, 11 Community Centre, Panchsheel Park,
New Delhi – 110 017, India
Penguin Group (NZ), cnr Airborne and Rosedale Roads, Albany, Auckland 1310,
New Zealand
(a division of Pearson New Zealand Ltd)
Penguin Books (South Africa) (Pty) Ltd, 24 Sturdee Avenue, Rosebank,
Johannesburg 2196, South Africa

Penguin Books Ltd, Registered Offices: 80 Strand, London WC2R 0RL, England

www.penguin.com

Published 2006
1

Text copyright © Nigel Crowle, 2006
Illustrations copyright © Martin Chatterton, 2006
All rights reserved

The moral right of the author and illustrator has been asserted

Set in Bookman Old Style
Made and printed in England by Clays Ltd, St Ives plc

British Library Cataloguing in Publication Data
A CIP catalogue record for this book is available from the British Library

ISBN-13: 978-0-141-32082-3
ISBN-10: 0-141-32071-0

This book is dedicated to my wife, Melanie, the real captain of the Crowle squad, and my son, Siôn, who's always Man of the Match in our eyes. (As ever, my playing position is Left Back in the changing rooms! That's if I'm picked at all!)

Traditional touchline support and encouragement came from Joan and Ken Crowle (or 'Mum and Dad', as the match programme refers to them).

Rhodri 'Bites Yer Legs' Crooks was a key player, due to his skill at volleying through those suggestions, stories and statistics. For that, I thank him very much.

For helping me out with odd facts, football books, statistics and general encouragement, I'd also like to thank my very able squad of players: Jane 'Head Hitter' Richardson; Rob 'Doug' Reynolds; Steve, Anna and Megan Davies; Paul 'Fella' Davies; Dr John 'Coach' Gibson and Sarah Manson.

Substitute Dexter Dog replaced Beverley Reynolds, who was ill – but at least she brought her own sick note.

Don't forget to flick the top right-hand corner of every page and see me play keepy-uppy!

Check out more fab facts at
www.know-it-all-guides.co.uk

Contents

So, You Want to Know about . . . Freaky Football

More people play it than any other game in the world! More people watch it than any other game in the world!

Some call it 'soccer', which comes from a shortened form of 'association', because 'association football' was the posh word for the glorious game. Some call it 'a kick-around in the park'. Whatever you call it, it's great fun to play and watch.

However, when you take a half-time break to get your breath back, you might want to have a quick flick through this book. You can use these **fabulous facts** in a number of different ways:

• You can **settle** arguments in playgrounds.

• You can even **shut up** big brothers or sisters who claim they know more than you about anything and everything – including football.

• You can **distract** adults when your mums and dads have just told you to tidy up your bedroom. Don't bother springing into action. Use the facts in this book to distract them – say 'Did you know...?' and add an amazing nugget of knowledge all about soccer.

But a word of warning. Every so often – among all these true facts – you'll find a fact that is complete tosh. An out-and-out lie. An outrageous falsehood. A load of balderdash, in fact!

So, that's your challenge – can you **Find That Fib** among these fabulously and fantastically fascinating footy facts? Read on, dear readers...

1. Football History

We don't know exactly who started the game, but we all agree that the football we know today began in England during the late 1800s. And so here are some facts about the history of footy, except one of them's totally untrue. Can YOU Find That Fib?

Really, Really Old Footballers

Around **255 BC**, the **Chinese** were probably the first people to come up with the idea of playing football. Some people say that they did this as a way of keeping soldiers fit between battles.

Tired warriors were kept on their toes by trying to slam some sort of spherical object, a *zuqiu* or football, between a hole in a net which was stretched between two bamboo poles. The game itself seems to have been called *Tsu Chu* – with *tsu* meaning 'using feet to kick a ball' and *chu* meaning 'a stuffed ball made of leather'. Archaeologists have uncovered evidence of ball games in **Egypt** taking place around **1800 BC**. These kick-about games were linked to religious ceremonies and fertility rites and large numbers of players took part. It is possible that these games were used as a means of churning up the soil and tilling it before sowing seeds for crops.

The **Aztecs** played a game in which a ball had to be pushed through holes 2.5 to 3 metres above the ground (a bit like a basketball hoop). They also came up with the idea of preserving the ball by putting it in a leather case and tying the laces together. Of course, we don't make footballs like that nowadays. That's because the leather soaked up any water on the pitch, making the ball really heavy. What's more, if you headed the ball, it did tend to leave a lace-hole imprint slap bang in the middle of your forehead! Even though the players wore protective gear, in the form of kneepads and helmets, it didn't help the losers. Defeated Aztec teams were often **sacrificed** to the gods!

Not to be outdone, the conquering **Romans** also claim to have started the modern game of football when they played *harpastum*. The Romans borrowed elements from an earlier Greek form of the game that used twelve players and a pitch to make it similar to our own soccer game. The addition of scrums and line-outs made the Roman version seem more of a cross between **rugby** and **American football**. The Romans themselves called

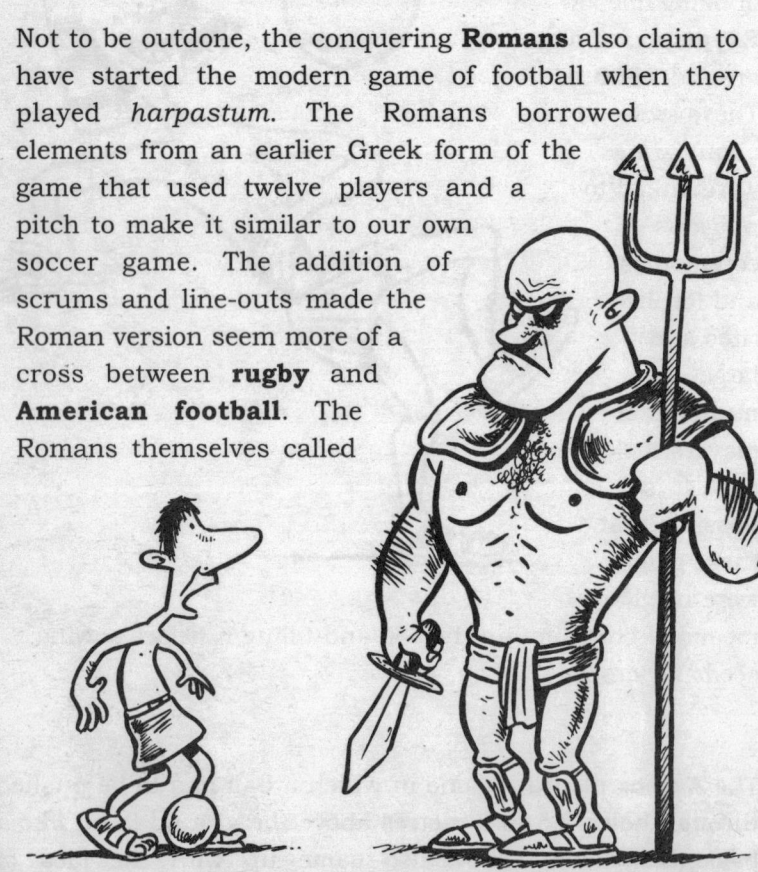

it the Small Ball Game, as they used much larger balls to play other games.

When the sun shone brightly, the **Vikings** used to play a type of football to praise their ancient sun god, Erik the Bright One. It was considered to be bad luck for a Viking warrior to remove his traditional **horned helmet** before a game, so any match was played with helmets jammed firmly on heads. As you'd expect, footballs got punctured as they landed on the sharp horns, which annoyed players on both sides. The Vikings came up with a solution – they played with footballs carved from wood. That stopped the balls bursting, but it did mean that Vikings who headed the ball were left with sore heads, despite their protective headgear. Often players had to be carried off the pitch, totally knocked out.

Around **AD 50**, the **Japanese** used to play a game called *kemari* which was like an ancient version of **keepy-uppy**. Using a 20-centimetre ball made of deerskin stuffed with sawdust, players kicked the ball as many times as they liked, keeping it up in the air and calling out, 'Ariyaa!' When the ball was passed on to other players, no tackling or physical contact were allowed and the player would shout, 'Ari!' That's why you'd hear players bellowing 'Ariyaa, ariyaa, ariyaa, ari!' until they got the ball back in their control. It was the ancient Japanese equivalent of one of today's players yelling, 'Go on, my son! 'Ave some of that!'

A little bit of cold weather shouldn't put you off playing footy. Ancient Inuit legends tell us that **Eskimos** believed that the spirits of their dead travelled to the **Northern Lights** where they played football for **eternity**. What's more, instead of a ball, they used the head of a walrus. Yuck!

Really, Really Old Footballers in Good Old Britain

In the UK, a game called *futeball* was played around the **twelfth century**. This early version of footy was a kind of free-for-all in which all the men **chased a ball** round a village or town boundary, up hill and down dale, with one aim in mind – to keep control of the ball by whatever means necessary. Getting a red card for a sending-off was the least of the players' worries. They had to avoid getting trampled or crushed and were happy to just survive a game!

By **1314**, England's **King Edward II** had banned a form of football with **500 players** on each side. The commoners who played the game weren't at all bothered, though. They carried on, even when subsequent kings – Edward III, followed by Richard II, Henry IV and Henry V – outlawed the game 'by pain of imprisonment' because they were worried that football was distracting people from all-important archery practice.

By the **nineteenth century**, a version of football became popular in the big posh schools of England. It was known as the **Cambridge Rules**, named after the university, and it became the basis of the modern game. However, around the same time, Rugby School created *its* own version of the rules for the game. Unlike the Cambridge Rules, players were allowed to pick up the ball and kick some shins as they played. During a meeting on 26 October 1863, officials from eleven London clubs and schools created a single set of rules to allow teams to play football against one another. This meeting created the **Football Association.** Rugby School's supporters had a huge row, left the meeting and split from the enthusiasts of 'association' football. The Rugby boys went off to make up rules and play their game, which was called 'netball'. Only joking! It was called 'rugby'.

Because handling the football was banned under the Cambridge Rules, players often had to wear gloves. This reminded them that they couldn't pick up the ball.

By the mid nineteenth century, football had become popular with the ordinary **working classes** and it was seen as a healthy, fun way of passing the time on a Saturday afternoon. In doing so, the workers turned football from a game for posh, rich kids into a game everyone could enjoy. **Football clubs** then sprang up all over the place.

Original Members of the Football League, Formed in 1888

Accrington	Aston Villa
Blackburn Rovers	Bolton Wanderers
Burnley	Derby County
Everton	Notts County
Preston North End	Stoke
West Bromwich Albion	Wolverhampton Wanderers

Quickie Quiz

Which of those original League members no longer exists today?

The answer is Accrington. The town of Accrington in Lancashire has an unhappy history when it comes to its football clubs. Accrington resigned from the Football League in 1893. A new club, called Accrington Stanley, played in the league from 1921 to 1962, then also resigned when it ran out of money. A new Accrington Stanley was formed in 1968 and by 2005 had worked its way back up the amateur leagues to the Nationwide Conference – one promotion away from getting back to the Football League. Maybe third time lucky!

2. Football Legends

This chapter lists some facts about those talented few whose special footy skills have dazzled us on the pitch. But be careful – don't YOU get dazzled by the one fact that's untrue amongst this lot. Can you Find That Fib? You'll be a legend yourself if you do!

When you're as nifty at the old game as me, you deserve a statue!

Famous Brit Footy Legends

Although **David Beckham** had worn the number 7 shirt for Manchester United and England, he was unable to wear it when he moved to **Real Madrid,** as teammate Raúl González Blanco had baggsed the right to wear that number in a written contract. Undaunted, Becks chose **23** instead – in tribute to the number worn by legendary Chicago Bulls basketball player **Michael Jordan**.

'The Welsh Wizard' **Ryan Giggs** played football for the England Schoolboys team when he was growing up in Manchester but he could only ever play footy at senior level for **Wales**. That's because he was born in Cardiff, in 1973, and has Welsh parents and grandparents. Giggsy's real surname is Wilson, but he was brought up by his mum and took her maiden name.

Incidentally, Real Madrid shirts bearing Beckham's name and new number sold out in Madrid on the day he completed his transfer. Nicknamed '**Golden Balls**' by newspaper reporters, Beckham puts on a **new** pair of football **boots** every game he plays. It's a custom that costs an estimated £300 a time.

Wayne Rooney was England's **youngest** player, aged 17 years and 111 days, when he made his debut against Australia in February 2003. He is also England's youngest-ever scorer.

Wayne Rooney,
aged 18 months.

Leslie Compton, aged 38 and 6 days, was the **oldest** player to make his England debut when he got the call-up against Wales in 1950. He was also a pretty handy cricketer, being the brother of cricket legend Dennis Compton.

Aged 40, Italian captain and goalie **Dino Zoff** was the oldest player to **win the World Cup** – that was when Italy won in 1982.

I say, old chap, this footie game's just not cricket...

Known for his breathtaking control of the ball and his brilliantly angled goals, flying winger **George Best** was arguably football's **first superstar**. Born in Northern Ireland, the late great George played for Manchester United during one of their many golden periods, and he won the award for European Player of the Year. During the **1960s,** when the Beatles were the biggest band in the world Georgie had his hair styled like the Fab Four and was even nicknamed 'El Beatle'. He liked to party and had girlfriends galore. As a result of his bad behaviour, Bestie served a prison term for drunken driving and assault.

12 Football Clubs that had George Best in their Team
(during the last ten years of his playing career)

1. Manchester United
2. Stockport County
3. Bournemouth
4. Fulham
5. Hibernian
6. Los Angeles Aztecs
7. Cork Celtic
8. Fort Lauderdale Strikers
9. San Jose Earthquakes
10. Dunstable Town
11. Brisbane Lions
12. Ford Open Prison

The **biggest England goalie** must have been the mighty **William Henry Foulke**, known to his friends as Fatty Foulke. He reached a hefty 152 kg (that's 24 stone), and was ace at stopping penalties. Being so heavy, he once **snapped the goal crossbar** while making a save – and stopped the game! He played in goal for Sheffield United during two winning FA Cup finals in 1899 and 1902. He also played for Chelsea, arriving one morning at the club's restaurant well before his teammates so that he could eat all eleven breakfasts! When he was injured during one game, it took six men to carry him off the pitch, and he was so heavy he broke the stretcher.

Former England captain and deadly striker **Gary Lineker** began his career at Leicester City before moving to clubs like Everton, Barcelona, Spurs and, finally, Nagoya Grampus Eight in Japan He always had a 'Mr Nice Guy' image and was **never cautioned** by a referee for foul play. Not once in his playing career did a referee give him even a yellow card, let alone a red one.

Gary retired from international football with 80 caps, having scored 48 goals – which is one less than the record-holder, Sir Bobby Charlton. He went on to munch crisps in adverts and point out footballing errors on BBC's *Match of the Day*. As Leicester's favourite son, Gary has been made a freeman of the city, which means he is allowed to go to the Town Hall Square and allow his sheep to graze. And, presumably, eat crisps there too.

Arsenal legend **Ian Wright** was their **top scorer** for six consecutive seasons in the 1990s. Since he stopped playing, he's become a top TV presenter . . . and he's also the adopted father of current England and Chelsea hotshot Shaun Wright-Phillips.

Now a top manager, **Mark Hughes** made his playing debut for Manchester United a few years before he actually signed for the Red Devils, when he was working as an **apprentice electrician** at the club. After fixing the bulbs in a set of floodlights, Mark took the opportunity to have a quick lunchtime kick around the empty Old Trafford pitch. One of Mark's kicks accidentally smashed into the floodlights he'd just fixed and the resulting power surge caused electricity supplies to be **blacked out** over half of Manchester. That's how he won the nickname of Sparky!

Young Football Player of the Year Award

Many players became legends from a young age, as this list shows. The PFA awards it to the most promising player in England under the age of twenty-three.

1976 – Peter Barnes (Manchester City)
1977 – Andy Gray (Aston Villa)
1978 – Tony Woodcock (Nottingham Forest)
1979 – Cyrille Regis (West Bromwich Albion)
1980 – Glenn Hoddle (Tottenham Hotspur)
1981 – Gary Shaw (Aston Villa)
1982 – Steve Moran (Southampton)
1983 – Ian Rush (Liverpool)
1984 – Paul Walsh (Luton Town)
1985 – Mark Hughes (Manchester United)
1986 – Tony Cottee (West Ham United)
1987 – Tony Adams (Arsenal)
1988 – Paul Gascoigne (Newcastle United)
1989 – Paul Merson (Arsenal)
1990 – Matthew Le Tissier (Southampton)
1991 – Lee Sharpe (Manchester United)
1992 – Ryan Giggs (Manchester United)
1993 – Ryan Giggs (Manchester United)
1994 – Andy Cole (Newcastle United)
1995 – Robbie Fowler (Liverpool)
1996 – Robbie Fowler (Liverpool)
1997 – David Beckham (Manchester United)
1998 – Michael Owen (Liverpool)
1999 – Nicolas Anelka (Arsenal)
2000 – Harry Kewell (Leeds United)
2001 – Steven Gerrard (Liverpool)
2002 – Craig Bellamy (Newcastle United)
2003 – Jermaine Jenas (Newcastle United)
2004 – Scott Parker (Chelsea)
2005 – Wayne Rooney (Manchester United)

Gazza's Top Five Daft Moments

During his playing heyday in the 1990s, Paul 'Gazza' Gascoigne was well known for being a bit of a joker...

5. Gazza once told an interviewer he was so superstitious about the number 13 that he simply couldn't bear to see the numbers 4 and 9 together. Strangely, he thought a combination of 5 and 8 was all right.

4. When his then manager Bobby Robson had called him 'daft as a brush', Gazza turned up for an England training session the next day with an actual brush sticking out of his sock.

3. Gazza once jumped on board a double-decker bus in London's Piccadilly Circus and astounded the passengers and the driver by asking if he could have a go at driving it. The bus driver agreed and the passengers claimed they thoroughly enjoyed Gazza's driving skills.

2. Gazza once astonished reporters in Rome by standing up at a press conference. He then asked for complete silence, before breaking wind really loudly!

1. When he was playing for Italian club Lazio, he was asked for a footballing comment and he burped enthusiastically into a TV microphone. That jokey belch cost Gazza a fine of £39,000.

Brazilian Footy Legends

Brazil can lay claim to being one of the world's greatest footballing nations, and here's the proof!

Pelé Power

Brazilian legend Pelé had an astonishing career. He led his club, Santos of São Paulo, to nine championship wins, and his Brazilian national team to three World Cup victories. During his 22-year career, he scored *1,282 goals* in *1,363 games*. This was second only to Arthur Friedenreich, another Brazilian player, who recorded 1,329 goals.

Pelé scored an average of one goal for every international match he played in, and during his best season (1958), he scored an amazing *139* times.

He also holds the record for hat-tricks (92) and the number of goals scored on the international level (97).

Four of Pelé's Nicknames
1. O' Rey (quite simply, 'The King')
2. Gasoline (due to his enormous energy)
3. The Executioner (for his superb moves on the pitch)
4. Black Pearl (because his talent was considered as rare as one of these)

Pelé's real name is Edson Arantes do Nascimento.

It's a Brazillian football tradition for stars to have their Christian name, rather than their surname, on the back of their shirt.

Brazilian football star **Ronaldo Luiz Nazario da Lima** was a **national hero** when Brazil beat Germany with a 2–0 **World Cup win** in **2002**. The 25-year-old won the Golden Boot Award for being top scorer of the tournament – 8 goals in 7 games, including the two that made the difference in the final. The win for Brazil – their fifth World Cup title – was all the more amazing because a terrible knee injury had prevented Ronaldo from playing football for the previous two years.

Brazil's captain, **Marcos Evangelista de Moraes Cafu**, also became the first player to appear in three successive finals.

Top Six Footballers' Bad Hair Days

Over the years, some footballers haven't exactly scored when it comes to haircuts. Here are the worst when it comes to footy fashion.

6. Ruud Guillit's Bad Dreadlocks

5. Kevin Keegan's Bubble-cut Perm

4. Chris Waddle's Permed Mullet

3. Jason Lee's Pineapple on His Head

2. Peter Beardsley's Pudding-basin Cut

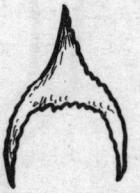

1. David Beckham's Mohican

3. Just for the Record

Use these astounding records wisely and you'll amaze people with your footy knowledge. However, be careful – one of these facts is totally made up and a load of nonsense. Can you pick it from the pack?

Famous Firsts

In **1860**, **Sheffield** became the first **northern working-class** side in the Football Association.

In **1871**, fifteen English teams and Scotland's Queen's Park took part in the first **FA Cup**. Played at London's Kennington Oval cricket ground in front of 2,000 spectators, the cup was won by a team of ex-university and public-schoolboy players called the Wanderers. They beat the Royal Engineers by one goal to nil.

The first official **England–Scotland international** was played in Glasgow in **1872.** The result was a goal-less draw.

The first **League and FA Cup double** was won by Preston North End. They won the first league championship in the **1888–9** season, and they won the FA Cup by beating Wolverhampton Wanderers 3–0.

Transfer Mania!

The first **£1,000** transfer fee was paid in 1905, when Alf Common moved from Sunderland to Middlesbrough.

The first **£10,000** transfer fee was paid in 1928, when David Jack moved from Bolton to Arsenal.

The first **£1 million** transfer fee was paid in 1979, when Trevor Francis moved from Birmingham City to Nottingham Forest.

The first **£10 million** transfer fee was paid in 1999, when Chris Sutton moved from Blackburn Rovers to Chelsea.

The world's first **non-white professional** footballer was **Arthur Wharton**, who became known as 'the best goalkeeper in the north' when, in the **1885–6** season, he played for Preston North End. Born in Ghana, of mixed-race parents, he was an all-round sportsman who helped overturn many Victorian prejudices. Shamefully overlooked by historians, Arthur played for Rotherham Town, among other northern clubs, before retiring from Stockport County in 1902. He died, without a penny to his name, in 1930.

The first **World Cup** was staged in Uruguay in **1930**. King Carol II of Romania was so keen on the tournament that he not only chose the players making up his country's team, but he also paid the travelling expenses of the twelve nations involved in the competition.

The first World Cup **England** took part in was in **1950**. It was remembered for a shock result in which an experienced English side lost 1–0 to an unfancied team from the USA.

The **referee's whistle** was introduced in **1878** at an FA Cup match between Nottingham Forest and Sheffield. Before that date, referees had to waggle a handkerchief around in front of players.

In **1965**, **Stanley Matthews** became the first footballer to receive a **knighthood**. His father, Jack, was a professional boxer, known as 'The Fighting Barber'. Sir Stan also holds the record for being the **oldest top-flight footballer** – he was still playing aged 50 years and 3 months.

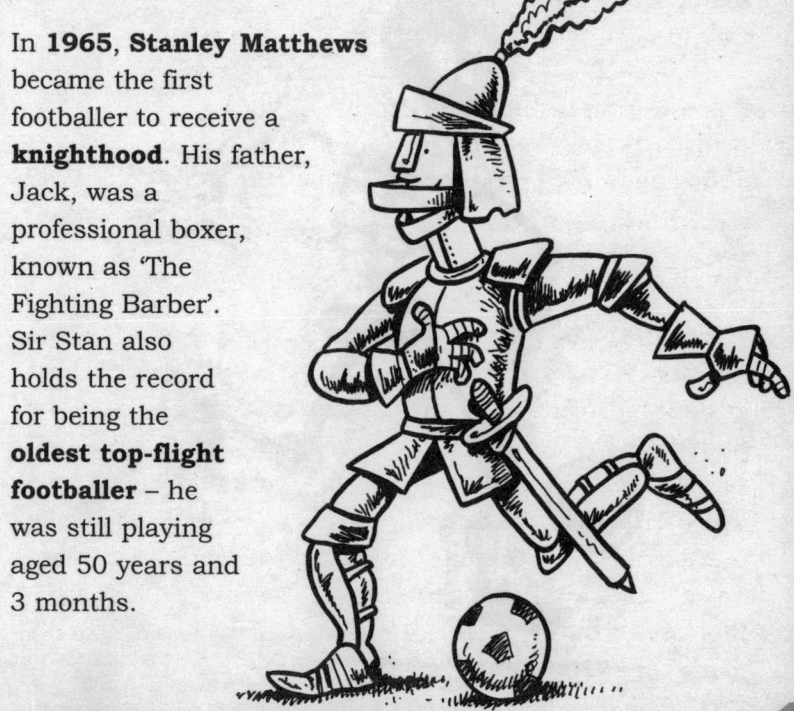

George Best was the first player to **score in a penalty shoot-out**. He scored for Manchester United against Hull City in the semi-final of the Watney Cup in **1970**. After the game ended 1–1, Best helped Man United win by 4 penalties to 3. One fact to please those many fans who dislike Man United – they went on to lose the final 4–1 to Derby County.

In **April 2005**, **Jermaine Pennant** became the first premiership player to wear an **electronic tag**. Pennant, who was wearing the tag while serving a three-month jail sentence for drink-driving, was cleared as being fit to play by the referee. Pennant didn't score, although his team, Birmingham, drew 1–1 at Newcastle.

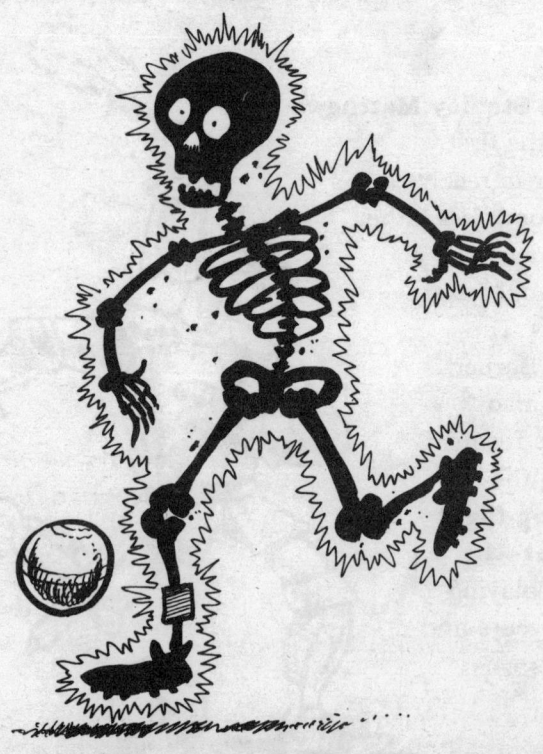

8 Amazing Firsts of the Original Wembley Stadium

1. The first live radio broadcast by a British king or queen was historically made from there in 1923, when King George V (Queen Elizabeth II's dad) opened the British Empire Exhibition.

2. The 1927 FA Cup final between Arsenal and Cardiff City was memorable for two things. Cardiff's Bluebirds took the cup out of England for the first and only time, when they beat the Gunners 1–0. The event was also noted as being the first time the crowd had sung the traditional Cup final hymn 'Abide With Me'.

3. In 1928, England suffered their first defeat at the old stadium when they lost 5–1 to the Scotland team, who became known as the 'Wembley Wizards'.

4. France earned a 2–2 draw in England's first international against foreign opponents at Wembley in 1945.

5. Tottenham completed the first League and Cup double at Wembley in 1961, when they beat Leicester City 2–0.

6. In 1963, Italy's AC Milan beat Portugal's Benfica 2–1 in Wembley's first European Cup final.

7. In 1965, West Ham won the first European Cup Winners Cup final to be played at Wembley. They won 2–1 against German side TSV Munich 1860.

8. A Wembley FA Cup final was drawn for the first time in 1970, when Chelsea and Leeds finished 2–2. Chelsea won the replay 2–1.

Record-breaking Moves

Doctors reckon that the reason **Wayne Rooney** is magic on the pitch is because he has brilliant **peripheral vision**. That's a scientific way of saying that Rooney can see sideways as he runs with the ball. It's a phenomenon known as **cross dominance**, where athletes like Rooney can coordinate ball skills just as easily between their left hand and eye, and their right hand and eye.

David Beckham's famous **banana-bending free kick** has been analysed by scientists. Their research, using high-speed cameras, showed that the ball initially travels at 129 km/h. It then spins counterclockwise at about eight revolutions per second, before swerving to the left. The ball rises up into the air and looks like it is about to soar over the goal's crossbar. Then it suddenly slows to 64 km/h, makes a sharp left turn, and drops into the top left corner of the net Gooooal!

In 1995, Colombian goalie **Rene Higuita** performed one of the most astonishing moves ever seen on a football pitch. After England's Jamie Redknapp had crossed the ball into Colombia's penalty area, goalie Higuita fell flat on his belly and arched his legs back over his body to give the ball what is now known as his trademark **scorpion kick** away from the goal-mouth. This move is so difficult that, when Preston Scout Leader and goalie Graham Alston later tried to copy Higuita by performing his own scorpion kick in a game, the poor chap ended up in hospital with a dislocated shoulder.

During the 1993–4 season of the Belgium championship, and in the last five minutes of the match, the goalie from AA Gent was sent off for a foul. Outfield player **Eric Viscaal** took his place and had to face the resulting **penalty kick**. Viscaal saved it, but then AA Gent still needed one goal to equalize. When AA Gent got a penalty kick in extra time, guess who took it and scored? Yep, stand-in goalie, amazing Eric!

In April 2004, amateur footballer **Marc Burrows** scored the world's **fastest goal straight from kick-off** – in just **2.5 seconds**! Marc was playing for Cowes Reserves in Sydenham's Wessex League when he hit the ball from the halfway line. Both teams watched in amazement as a strong gust of wind carried the ball over the head of the other team's keeper.

The previous fastest goal was scored in 2.8 seconds by Argentinian player Ricardo Olivera in 1998.

On the Ball

All sorts of ordinary people have set extraordinary records.

Keepy-Uppy
The current world record-holder for keepy-uppy is Nikolai Kutsenko of Ukraine who set the record of **24 hours and 30 minutes** in 1997. That's over one whole day juggling a ball without it ever touching the ground.

Dr Jan Skorkovsk *ran* the **Prague City Marathon** (that's *42.195 km*) while keeping a football continuously in the air. He did this on 8 July 1990, finishing in a time of **7:18:55 hours**.

Agim Agushi from Kosovo **walked 15.356 km** while heading a football in just over **three hours** on 27 October 2002 in Munich, Germany.

Welsh schoolgirls and sisters Anna and Megan Davies hold the national record for the number of times they **headed** a football between themselves – an astonishing **1,928 headers** during a **two-hour** session in Cardiff in 2002

Quickie Quiz
Arguably the **best World Cup goal** was in 1986, when England played Argentina. After a handball incident – which he claimed was due to the 'Hand of God' – who scored after a brilliant run from his own half? Was it:

a) Maradona?
b) Madonna?
c) Macarena?

The answer's a) Maradona – Diego Maradona – who's now one of the stars of an Argentinian version of the TV show Strictly Come Dancing.

In April 2005, **amateur** footballer Ryan Smith **scored 16 goals** when his Grimsby club, the Expressions Colts, beat Holton Le Clay Grasshoppers by 20 goals to nil. Ryan broke the **scoring record** for the Lincolnshire Intermediate Football League, and he's looking to get his fantastic feat recognized as a world individual scoring record in an authorized football match.

4. Freaky Injuries

Some of footy's finest players can be awfully accident-prone. Here's a selection of some of the stranger footballing injuries that have occurred over the years. Mind you, there's still a whopping great lie waiting to trip you up and cry 'Foul'. Can you Find That Fib?

On the Pitch

As Arsenal celebrated on the Wembley pitch after winning the 1993 Coca-Cola Cup final, **Steve Morrow** was picked up by his jubilant captain, Tony Adams, who proceeded to put poor Steve over his shoulder. Unfortunately, the skipper dropped Steve, who hit the ground and broke his **arm.**

Manchester City goalie **Bert Trautman** broke his **neck** during the 1956 FA Cup final. A courageous Bert still played on for the last fifteen minutes. In case you're wondering, Man City won 3–1.

Trautman was actually German and had been captured during the **Second World War** and held in a British prisoner of war camp. In 2004 Herr Trautman was awarded the OBE for his efforts to improve British–German relations.

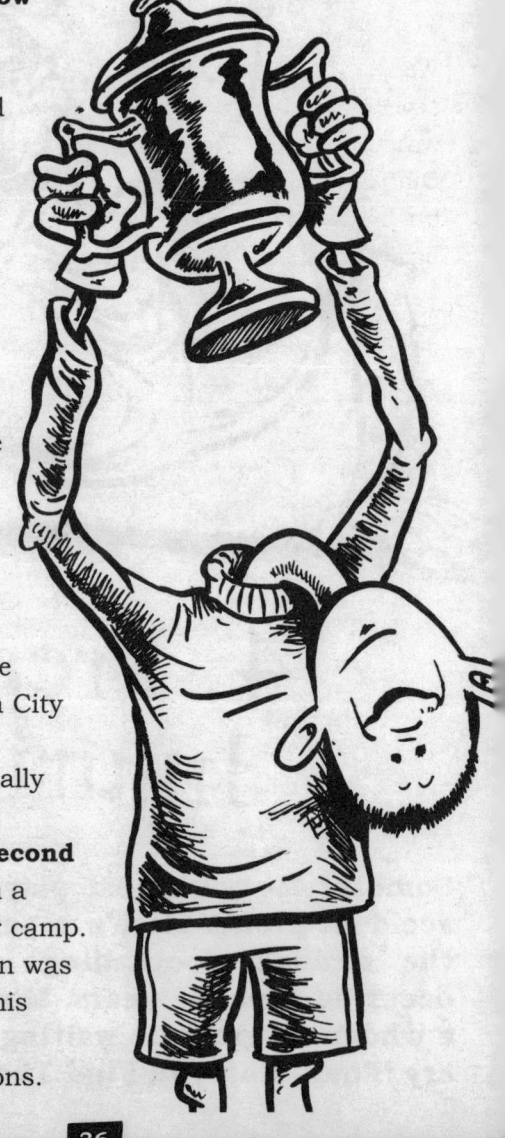

In 1975, Manchester United goalie **Alex Stepney** got really worked up as he yelled encouragement to his teammates in a game against Birmingham City. In fact, Alex screamed so hard that he dislocated his **jaw** and had to leave the pitch!

Welsh international goalkeeper **Andy Dibble** suffered severe **chest burns** from sliding along the grass when he was playing for Barry Town against Carmarthen in 2003. Dibble, who had to have a skin graft, believed that the burns were caused by a chemical called hydrated lime that had been used to mark the penalty spot.

Arsenal striker **Thierry Henry** struck a spell of bad luck in 2004. The French international made a blistering run up the left-hand side of the pitch in a game against Chelsea, and seemed certain to score. However, the groundsman had carelessly propped his brush up against an advertising hoarding. As the hoarding electronically rotated, the brush fell over . . . right in the path of a thundering Thierry. He **tripped** and had to be taken off for treatment. Not so much 'Va Va Voom!' as 'Uh oh! Broom!'

In 1987, Torquay United were playing at home to Crewe in their final Division Four game. Torquay needed to win to avoid being relegated to the Conference, but found themselves trailing 2–1. When the game was almost over, suddenly, Torquay player **Jim McNichol** was **bitten on the upper thigh** by a police **dog** called Bryn, who was patrolling the touchline with his handler. It took four minutes to patch up the wound, and in the fourth minute of injury time Torquay striker Paul Dobson grabbed the dramatic equalizer that Torquay needed to stay up.

Quickie Quiz
In a new season, can you guess what a footballer is most likely to strain? Is it a:
(a) hamstring?
(b) ham bone?
(c) ham sandwich?

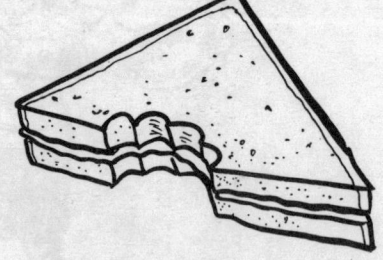

The answer, of course, is a hamstring: 20 per cent of footballers' first injuries of the season happen to their hamstrings. These are the muscles in the upper part of the leg, or thigh, which get harmed when players try to sprint across a pitch.

Off the Pitch

Eye Injuries

'The Battle of the Boot' took place in the Old Trafford changing rooms in February 2003. Manchester United had just lost 2–0 to Arsenal, and manager **Sir Alex Ferguson** wasn't happy. As he told his players just how unhappy he was, Sir Alex kicked a boot, which went flying towards captain **David Beckham**, hitting him above the eye. Sir Alex explained the accident away as a 'freak act of nature'. Beckham, however, was more than a little miffed, as he needed stitches for the injury.

Danish footy star **Allan Nielson** had to miss three games for Tottenham Hotspur after his newborn daughter poked him in the eye.

Croatian striker **Milan Rapaic** missed the start of the season for his club, Hajduk Split, after sticking his boarding pass in his eye at the airport.

Watching TV

Expensive defender **Rio Ferdinand** managed to injure himself watching TV in 2001, causing him to miss at least two games for Leeds. Ferdinand strained a tendon behind his knee while he was resting his foot on a coffee table and watching the box.

It's easily done, though. Towards the end of his playing career with Liverpool, **Robbie Fowler** also managed to give himself a severe knee strain with the simple act of stretching forward to reach a TV remote-control unit.

Leg and Feet Injuries

Goalkeeper **Dave Beasant** was out of action for eight weeks in 1993 after he dropped a large bottle of salad cream on his foot, severing the tendon in his big toe.

England's tough-guy midfielder **David Batty** re-injured his Achilles tendon when his own toddler bashed into him on a tricycle.

Barnsley's **Darren Barnard** found himself on the sidelines for a full five months with a torn knee ligament. He accidentally slipped in a puddle of his puppy's pee on the kitchen floor.

Santiago Canizares – the **Valencia** player who was Spain's premier goalkeeper – couldn't play in the 2002 World Cup after he accidentally stepped on a broken bottle of aftershave. A shard of glass cut a tendon in his foot.

Just Being Plain Stupid

In 1988, **American** goalkeeper **Kasey Keller** managed to knock out his front teeth, simply by pulling his golf clubs out of the boot of his car.

Arsenal player **Perry Groves** leapt to his feet while celebrating a goal. Nothing unusual there, you might say. However, he'd forgotten he was sitting in the dug-out at the time and only watching the game from the touchline. In fact, the hapless Perry knocked himself out on the dug-out's roof and had to receive medical treatment.

In the 1970s, **Norwegian** international defender **Svein Grondalen** had to withdraw from a match after having an accident while he was out jogging. He collided with a moose.

4. Oi, Ref!

There's always got to be someone on the pitch who fans love to hate during a football game. Usually, that 'someone' is the referee, or the Bloke in Black. Read some of these fab facts about refs . . . and watch out – you might get red-carded if you don't Find That Fib!

Normally, footy referees are keen to make sure that players don't swear and lose their temper when playing – especially when it's at amateur level.

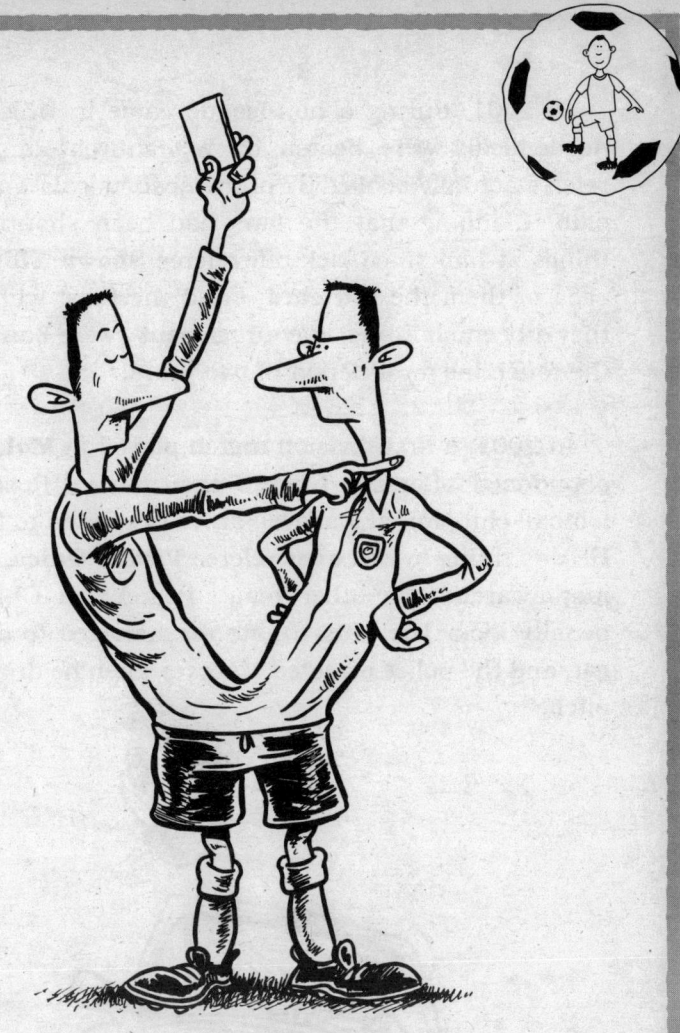

A 2005 Sunday League game between **Peterborough North End** and **Royal Mail** was abandoned when, 63 minutes into the game the referee sent **himself** off! Ref **Andy Wain** lost his temper, threw his whistle on the ground and stormed over to the unfortunate North End goalie who had disagreed with Andy's decision. 'If a player did that, I would send him off, so I had to go,' said referee Andy. He showed himself the red card and ordered himself off the pitch!

In 2001, during a non-league game in which Totnes Academicals were beaten by Whitchurch Rangers, the referee actually booked 37 of the Academicals' supporters' club. Claiming that the fans had been shouting nasty things at him since kick-off, referee **Shawn Ellis** showed each of them the **red card** – and the fans, who claimed they'd been shouting 'encouragement', were **banned** from the touchline for a period of two years.

In 2004, a first-division match played in **Moldova** was abandoned after the furious chairman of Roso Floreni football club, Mihai Macovei, drove his car on to the pitch. He was trying to **run over** referee **Vitalie Onica**, who had just awarded the other team, Politehnica Chisinau, a penalty kick. The unfortunate ref managed to dodge the car, and the police arrested Macovei when he drove off the pitch.

Referees sometimes do the strangest things. In 2001, in an Essex amateur match between Wimpole 2000 and Earls Colne Reserves, referee **Brian Savill** decided to give the losing Wimpole 2000 a helping hand. He volleyed the ball into the back of the net from a corner and **scored a goal**. Wimpole were actually 18–1 down before Mr Savill decided to have a go at goal. It made little difference, as Earls Colne managed to cling on for an eventual 20–2 win. However, the FA charged Savill with bringing the game into disrepute, and gave him a seven-week ban. Savill resigned in protest at their lack of sense of humour.

Top Three Quickest Red Card Incidents

3. The dubious record of the Fastest Sending-Off in British football is held by former **Sheffield Wednesday** goalkeeper **Kevin Pressman**. He was sent off after just thirteen seconds for handling a shot from **Wolverhampton's Temuri Ketsbaia** outside the area during the opening weekend of the 2001 season.

2. On 9 December 1990, Italian footballer **Giuseppe Lorenzo**, who played for Bologna, was sent off after just ten seconds for hitting another player during a league match against Parma.

1. In a match against Darlington, substitute and Jamaican international **Walter Boyd** came on just as a free kick was waiting to be taken. Then he punched an opponent before play had restarted. Referee Clive Wilkes sent Boyd off, and so – as Clive hadn't restarted his watch – Boyd's stay on the pitch lasted **zero seconds**. It's the official world record for the **quickest-ever red card**. It can never be beaten, and is unlikely to ever be equalled.

Clive Wilkes paid £75 to a blacksmith to make a special weathervane to commemorate the record. It was a cut-out of a referee showing someone a red card. This unusual weathervane still whirls proudly round on the roof of his house.

In another game, Celtic player Tommy Burns was sent off by the referee **after** he'd been substituted. It seems that naughty Tommy said something rude to the ref as he left the pitch, shook hands with the player coming on, and headed for the tunnel. The ref called him back and gave his second yellow card of that match. Celtic were allowed to carry on with eleven men because Burns had already been substituted.

While playing for Rangers in Scotland, **Paul Gascoigne** noticed that referee **Dougie Smith** had dropped his **yellow card** on the pitch. For a joke, Gazza showed the ref the yellow card as if he was booking him. The ref didn't see the funny side and booked Gazza for real.

6. Footy Fans

Ah, the loyal fans of football. The ones who stand around muddy pitches, or even just lounge in front of *Match of the Day*. The beautiful game would be nothing without their enthusiasm. However, are you as enthusiastic when it comes to Finding That Fib?

Romanian football fan Ghita Axinte was so angry when his team lost a World Cup qualifier against the Czech Republic, he hurled his **TV set** through the window of his flat! Unfortunately, neighbour Radu Demergiu was sitting on the balcony just below, but narrowly avoided the flying TV. 'He could have killed us,' said a forgiving Demergiu. 'But when he told me he'd been watching the football, I completely understood.'

There are an estimated 40 million **Manchester United** fans in **Asia** alone.

Apparently, a man and woman who were Gooners – that is, two completely bonkers **Arsenal** fans – once named their child 'Lanesra'. (Tip: Read it backwards!)

The yellow **Brazil shirt** that had been worn by the legendary **Pelé** during the 1970 World Cup final was auctioned recently. The bids reached a staggering £157,750 before being bought by one lucky fan.

In 2005, **Swansea City** moved from the Vetch Field to its new Morfa ground. Over the years, around 50 urns containing the **ashes** of dead Swans supporters had been buried under the old pitch. Families had the option of having the urns dug up and moved to the new ground.

Bristol City fan Jer Boon managed to combine his love of cycling with his love of his club. To raise money for a cancer charity, Jer **cycled** to every one of his team's home and away games in the 2003–4 season and reckons he's raised £10,000. He cycled 8,606 miles, braving gales, snow and heavy rain. However, his season ended in disappointment when Bristol City lost 1–0 to Brighton and Hove Albion in the Division Two play-offs.

When Scottish fan Calum Best (no relation of George) was thrown out of a Norwegian pub, called 'The Scotsman', for playing his **bagpipes** in support of his team, the travelling Scottish fans got all huffy and decided to drink elsewhere too. Now, when they go on tour, they visit another pub in Oslo – 'The Dubliner'! – where Calum can play his bagpipes to his heart's content!

In September 2005, 289 **Gambian** football fans travelling by plane persuaded their pilots to request an **emergency landing** in Peru. The pilots claimed the jet was low on fuel. However, the real reason was so that the football-crazy passengers could watch their nation's team play against Qatar in the FIFA Under-17 World Championships. Gambia won 3–1.

Gambia's result was a run-way success.

Footy Chants

If you disagree with the ref's decision, any team can sing (to the tune of 'Three Blind Mice'):

'Three blind refs,
Three blind refs!
See how they run!
See how they run!
Their whistles are stuck,
And their eyes are closed!
What they call, nobody knows!
Three blind refs,
Three blind refs!'

If you want to make fun of other clubs, sing along to the tune of 'Land of Hope and Glory'. Here's Man U's version:

'We hate Nottingham Forest,
We hate Everton too,
We hate Manchester City,
But . . . United we love you!'

(Feel free to change the names of clubs!)

When Gerard Houllier was manager of Liverpool, fans in the Kop end of the ground sang to the tune of 'Who Let the Dogs Out?':

'Hou let the Reds out? Hou-Hou-Houllier!
Hou let the Reds out? Hou-Hou-Houllier!'

Also, to the tune of The Beatles' 'Yellow Submarine', fans sing:

'We all live in a red and white Kop,
A red and white Kop,
A red and white Kop . . .'

(And they repeat the lines forever . . .)

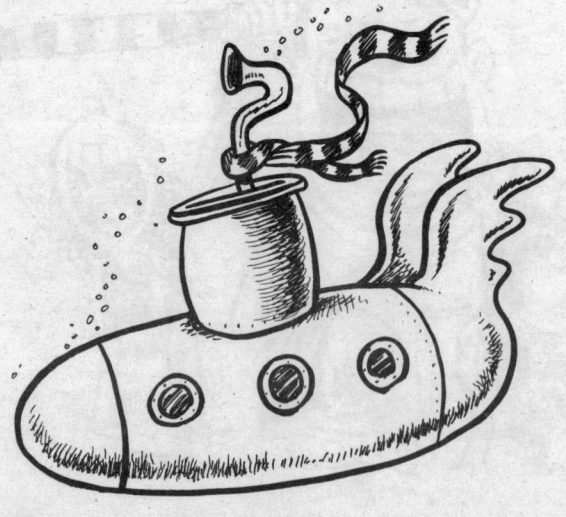

Here's one that everyone chants about Millwall Football Club:

**'We hate Millwall and we hate Millwall,
We hate Millwall and we hate Millwall!
We are the Millwall Haters!'**

Hundreds of years ago, German classical composer Ludwig van Beethoven wrote one of Germany's most popular chants. To the tune of his famous *Fifth Symphony* – the one that goes 'Duh duh duh daaaa!' – he wrote in German lyrics which translate as:

**'You're going to lose . . .
You're going to lose . . .'**

Here's one, sung to the tune of 'Camptown Races', that naughty England fans sing whenever they play Germany:
'Two World Wars and one World Cup . . . Doo-dah, doo-dah!'

Fans of Welsh wizard Ryan Giggs often chant the following song during Manchester United games, sung to the tune of the old *Robin Hood* TV theme:

'Ryan Giggs, Ryan Giggs, running down the wing,
Ryan Giggs, Ryan Giggs, can do anything,
Feared by the Blues, loved by the Reds,
Ryan Giggs, Ryan Giggs, Ryan Giggs.'

Newcastle fans, overjoyed that Michael Owen has joined the club, sing to the tune of 'Michael Row the Boat Ashore':

'Michael Owen scores our goals, hallelujah!
Michael Owen scores our goals, hallelujah!'

Liverpool fans shout the praises of their 6 foot 7 striker by singing:

'He's big,
He's red,
His feet stick out the bed
Peter Crouch, Peter Crouch!'

7. Home Ground

It's time to look at some cold, hard facts about clubs and stadiums. But, be careful – one of the following facts is completely made up. Can you manage to Find That Fib?

Stadium Statistics

The original **Wembley Stadium** was built on a base of 25,000 tons of concrete to support the foundations and the outside walls. It took a year to build, and the stadium was finished just three days before the first FA Cup final at the ground. There is a rumour that one of the narrow-gauge trains used to transport materials in and out of the site is buried under the arena.

Top Three Goals Scored at Old Wembley Stadium
Before historic old Wembley was demolished, football fans were asked to look back over 77 years and decide the best goal ever scored at the stadium.

3. Third place goes to **Sir Geoff Hurst**'s classic hat-trick goal in the 1966 World Cup final.

2. In second place is the goal scored by Spurs winger **Ricky Villa** for his amazing dribble through Manchester City's defence in the 1981 FA Cup final.

1. Paul Gascoigne won the award for his goal against Scotland in the first round of the 1996 European championships. Receiving the ball outside the box, Gazza cheekily flicked it over the head of the last Scottish defender as he ran past him, then smashed a volley past Scotland's goalie Andy Goram to put England 2–0 ahead.

The **world's biggest** football stadium is **the Maracana** in **Brazil**. Looking a bit like a massive **spaceship**, it was built for the 1950 World Cup. In that year's final – Brazil v Uruguay – almost 200,000 extremely excitable South American footy fans filled every inch of the stadium. Sadly for Brazil, they lost 2–1.

The Maracana stadium has plenty of atmosphere.

The new **Wembley National Stadium** has seating for over 90,000 fans, which makes it the world's biggest fully-covered football stadium.

Wolverhampton Wanderers' **Molineux Stadium** was the first major British ground to be able to host games at night after **floodlights** were fitted in 1953. That's probably why the Wolves players wore luminous satin kit to catch the light when they played their first game against a touring side from South Africa. Other football clubs followed Wolves's lead and installed floodlights. Fans loved night games, but cinema owners weren't happy – they reckoned that cinema takings went down as a result.

Stockholm's Djurgardens FC play in a magnificent domed stadium built in the shape of a **horseshoe** for Sweden's hosting of the 1912 Olympic Games. If you don't like the football, you can always marvel at the intricate walrus heads carved into the walls.

Manchester United's **Old Trafford** stadium is one of the best-known grounds in the world. It was opened in 1910, having cost £60,000 to build. Sir Bobby Charlton memorably called it the 'Theatre of Dreams' because he'd seen or played in so many of the Glorious Game's glorious games there.

Old Trafford was the **most bombed** football ground during the Second World War, and was awarded over £22,000 to rebuild its main stand and pitch.

Clubs

Locations of Arsenal Football Clubs
(in places other than Highbury, UK)

1. You'll find Arsenal Futbol Club in Buenos Aires, Argentina.

2. Gunners LC play in the lower depths of the Belgian football league.

3. Arsenal Tula play in Russia.

4. Arsenal Amsterdam are a Dutch side.

5. Canada boasts a Saskatoon Arsenal.

6. Arsenal Guadeloupe play in the West Indies.

7. In the South African kingdom of Maseru, a group of Arsenal fans founded Arsenal Lesotho. Their nickname is also 'The Gunners' and they too play in a red and white strip. What's more, in the years 1989 and 1991, both Arsenal and Arsenal Lesotho won the League and Cup double.

When American businessmen, the Glazer brothers – Bryan, Avi and Joel, bought **Manchester United**, they were so **puzzled** by the rules of the game that they had to get translators to explain the game to them.

Quickie Quiz

Test your footy knowledge with these quick questions.

1. Which club began life as Dial Square in 1886: Arsenal or Chelsea?

The answer's Arsenal, which changed its name to Royal Arsenal in 1891, Woolwich Arsenal in 1896, before finally becoming just plain old 'Arsenal' in 1913.

2. Which club began life as the Black Arabs in 1883: Bristol Rovers or Wolverhampton Wanderers?

The answer's Bristol Rovers, which changed its name from the Black Arabs in 1898.

3. Which club began playing as St Jude's in 1885: Ipswich Town or Queen's Park Rangers?

The answer's Queen's Park Rangers, which made its name change in 1887.

Everton and Liverpool

Rivalry between **Everton** and **Liverpool** dates as far back as 1891, and arose because of a dispute about footy grounds. In those days, Everton used to play their games at Anfield, which today is home to Liverpool. But when the landowner, **John Houlding**, put up the rent he charged Everton to play there, the club's members objected and decided to build a new ground nearby, **Goodison Park**, where Everton still play today. Left with a football ground but no team to play there, an angry Houlding sneakily registered the name 'Everton' and set up a new club to play under that name at Anfield. But because the Football Association ruled that there couldn't be two clubs called Everton, Houlding changed the name of his new club to Liverpool. And so one of England's fiercest football rivalries began.

Name Game Quiz

There may well be 92 clubs in the Football League, but only four of them have names that begin and end with the same letter. Can you name them?

They are Aston Villa, Charlton Athletic, Liverpool and Northampton Town.

Quickie Quiz

What word links the following clubs?

Airdrie	Ayr	Boston
Carlisle	Colchester	Hartlepool
Leeds	Manchester	Newcastle
Oxford	Peterborough	Rotherham
Scunthorpe	Sheffield	Southend
Torquay	West Ham	

The word is 'United', the name a club takes on when two merge.

West Bromwich Albion has two nicknames. They used to be known as '**The Throstles**', 'throstle' being what Black Country locals called a thrush. Thrushes were common in the hawthorn bushes around the ground. Nowadays, West Brom are known as '**The Baggies**', a nickname which probably refers to the fashion in past years for footy players to wear really baggy shorts.

Three Everton Nicknames

1. They are '**The Blues**', after their distinctive strip of royal-blue shirts and white shorts.

2. They are also known as '**The Toffees**'. A local sweet shop – Mother Noblett's Toffee Shop – advertised Everton mints on match days. That's why a match-day tradition was the Toffee Lady, who walked round the pitch, chucking Everton mints into the crowd.

3. Everton were originally known as '**The Black Watch**', because when players from other teams joined the club wearing their old kit, to save confusion on match days players' kit was dyed black.

Two of Scotland's clubs are called **Forfar** and **East Fife**. For years football fans have eagerly waited every time these two teams meet to see if the result ends in the tongue-twister 'Forfar 4, East Fife 5'. Sadly, it hasn't yet, the nearest being in the 1963–4 season, when the match ended Forfar 5, East Fife 4.

The **Ivory Coast** national football team are nicknamed 'The Elephants'.

In 2006 they packed their trunks for Germany and their first appearance in a World Cup.

Quickie Quiz

Name the football clubs associated with these animal nicknames:

1. The Foxes
2. The Owls
3. The Magpies
4. The Robins
5. The Seagulls
6. The Lions
7. The Tigers
8. The Swans
9. The Wolves
10. The Canaries
11. The Eagles
12. The Terriers
13. The Gulls

1. Leicester City
2. Sheffield Wednesday
3. Both Notts County and Newcastle United are known as 'The Magpies'
4. This nickname is shared by three clubs – Bristol City, Cheltenham Town and Swindon Town
5. Brighton and Hove Albion
6. Millwall
7. Hull City
8. Swansea City
9. Wolverhampton Wanderers
10. Norwich City
11. Crystal Palace
12. Huddersfield Town
13. Torquay United

But the best nickname of all has to be Northampton Town's, which is 'Cobblers'!

Get Your Kit On!

Back in 1979, **Liverpool**'s Hitachi shirt was the first sponsored shirt to be worn by a professional British football club.

Portsmouth's away kit in the 1989–91 season was a tribute to – some would say a direct copy of – Brazil's distinctive colours. They wore yellow shirt, blue shorts and green and yellow trim on white socks.

The Mexico World Cup of 1994 was brightened up considerably every time goalie **Jorge Campos** took to the field. He'd designed his own kit – a crazy mix of black and green stripes over red and yellow zigzags. Other neon-coloured favourites include purple and yellow splodges, and a pink, yellow, green and purple diamond outfit.

Hull City are a club known as the **Tigers**. Which is why their marketing department decided they should wear a special tiger-striped kit for their 1990–91 season.

The name's Toucan. PeeTee Toucan...

Mascot Antics

Partick Thistle's mascot is Pee Tee, the Toucan. It's become a tradition for famous fans of Partick Thistle to wear the brightly coloured psychedelic outfit and dance around to please the crowd. Among the celebrities who have worn the Pee Tee Toucan outfit over the years are members of top Scottish pop group Franz Ferdinand, comedian Billy Connolly and Hollywood superstar Sir Sean Connery.

In 2002, in a Grand National race for football mascots, **Chaddy the Owl** – proud supporter of **Oldham Athletic** – romped home in first place. However, **Scunthorpe United's Scunny Bunny** wasn't happy, and he made a complaint that Chaddy's **boots** weren't as big as the pantomime-style whoppers worn by the other mascots. But officials were happy to let the result stand.

Hartlepool United Football Club are nicknamed the **Monkey Hangers** by their rivals. Hartlepool's residents are famously said to have hanged a monkey during the Napoleonic Wars because they thought it was a French spy. In May 2002, the town's football club mascot H'Angus the Monkey was elected Mayor of Hartlepool. H'Angus, known in real life as Stuart Drummond, landed the job with the slogan 'Free bananas for schoolchildren!'

Top Three Mascots Named After Famous Footballing Legends

3. Lofty the Lion, Bolton's mascot, is named after the legendary Nat Lofthouse.

2. Cardiff City's Bartley Bluebird is named after Bartley Wilson, the founder of Riverside FC, which went on to become Cardiff City.

1. Luton's Happy Harry is named after the club's famous former manager, one 'Happy' Harry Haslam.

Bristol City's Cat has been involved in a rather embarrassing incident. He got the red card on his first trip out at City's home ground, Ashton Court, when he skipped on to the pitch waving wildly to young fans – only to find that his shorts had fallen down.

8. Strange But True

This starting line-up of more strange stories should test you and see if you're match-fit when it comes to Finding That Fib.

Elephants on the Pitch

In January 2004, in **India**, almost **100 elephants** took part in a series of **football games** in an annual festival to encourage locals to protect the creatures. Up to 10,000 fans watched the first match at the three-day event, which was staged at the Kaziranga National Park.

Later in 2004, **Thailand**'s head of the prison service organized a match between his **prisoners' team** and a rival team of **ten football-playing elephants** in a bid to discourage prisoners from gambling on football results. The game is reported to have ended in a 5–5 draw, although **muddy conditions** meant that some supporters couldn't see when the ball crossed the goal line and thought the elephants triumphed by 7 goals to 6. Trainer Pattarapon Meepan said, 'Elephants are not the best players because they are quite slow. We train them every day to keep them from treading on the other players.'

Leicester City scored a memorable 10–0 win over Portsmouth in the late 1920s. The goal feast was largely due to one of their legendary players, their record goalscorer Arthur Chandler. After he'd scored his sixth goal, the crowd were amazed to see six swans flying over the Filbert Street ground. Six goals, six swans – strange coincidence, or what?

At the first **Wembley Cup final** in **1923**, 200,000 fans turned up when there was only room on the terraces for 127,000. Billy, a **thirteen-year-old police horse**, and his rider PC George Scorey became the heroes of the day, pushing thousands of fans who were on the pitch back to stand on the touchlines so that the game could begin. The match became known as the 'White Horse Final'.

Birmingham City's St Andrew's pitch was said to be **cursed by gypsies** who were angry at being thrown off the land to make way for the stadium. When the team were suffering a run of bad results he couldn't explain, Birmingham manager **Barry Fry** consulted an expert on witchcraft, who told him he could lift the curse by **peeing** on every corner of the pitch before games. Fry duly relieved himself, and the Blues's results quickly improved!

Officials were quick to react when teams complained about the **unlucky changing rooms** at **Cardiff's Millennium Stadium**. Eleven teams in all, including Chelsea, Arsenal and Spurs, blamed their match losses as a direct result of having used the south changing rooms at the stadium. Bosses brought in a top artist to paint a lucky two-metre-high sun mural on the wall . . . and now the south changing rooms one is considered jinx-free.

Preston North End's centre forward had a rather unusual habit – he used to enjoy walking his **pet fox** on the pitch at **half-time**. Why he did it, no one knows – in fact, you might say he had everyone 'foxed'!

When **David and Victoria Beckham** failed to appear on an American TV chat show in July 2004, the show's producers found a suitable replacement. Mr and Mrs Beckham's TV interview spot was filled by a pair of **performing seals**.

Stacked heels and platform soles first became hugely popular in the 1970s. Back in 1972, **Burnley Football Club** actually turned out for a match wearing **green football boots** with a 7.**5cm stacked heel and a 5cm platform sole**. Unfortunately, coach John Gibson made the side change back to normal black footy boots at half-time because four players fell over and twisted their ankles during the first half.

When Liverpool won the Champions League in 2005, **Steven Gerrard** told the newspapers that he slept with the trophy in his hotel bedroom. He said, 'I did not want to let it out of my sight. When someone took it away from me, it felt as though somehow I had lost a part of me.'

When Celtic goalie **John Thomson** collided with a forward playing for deadly rivals **Glasgow Rangers** in 1931, he was hurt so badly he tragically died later. However, his fame lives on with Celtic's **spooky chant**, which includes the lines: 'Between your posts, there stands a ghost!'

Even though she died back in 1609, the ghost of **Lady Elizabeth Hoby** has been spotted by many of the **England squad** during their visits to England's team headquarters at **Bisham Abbey**. Stories are told that she slips out of her painting, which hangs in the Great Hall, and goes walkabout! She always looks sad, which some say is due to her feeling guilty about one of her six children dying after she locked him in a small room and forgot about him!

The ghost of famous English naval hero **Admiral Lord Horatio Nelson** apparently haunts the boardroom at **Blackpool Football Club**. It's not because old Horatio was a

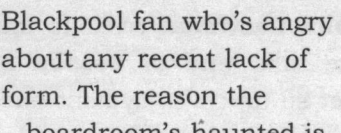

Blackpool fan who's angry about any recent lack of form. The reason the boardroom's haunted is because the walls are made of panels of **wood** from one of **Nelson's flagships**. It seems the club's Labrador dog gets all twitchy when it roams round that boardroom, and starts barking at the walls!

Those Wacky International Teams

What sort of problems have fourth-division Romanian football club Steau Nicolae Balcescu been experiencing recently? Have they:

1. Run out of footballs?
2. Run out of strength to kick footballs?
3. Had to dodge fans fighting on the terraces and the football pitch?

The answer is 3. Apparently, Steau Nicolae Balcescu FC was warned that if it did not stop its fans fighting on the terraces and invading the pitch, it would be kicked out of the Romanian league. So they came up with a solution: they've encircled their pitch with a crocodile-filled moat.

Expert **Dr John Castleton** reckons that many fans suffer from what he calls '**end of Season Affective Disorder**'. Those fans get so much enjoyment out of supporting their teams that they get really depressed when there are no games to watch. That's why, in 2003, the good doctor set up a **phone line** that plays a recording of football crowd noises to help 'SAD' fans.

Quickie Quiz

Why did Dutch non-league side **Putbroek Football Club** cover their football pitch with **human hair**? Was it:

1. The latest crowd-control tactic?
2. Because they'd torn out their hair in frustration at losing?
3. Their ground was next to a hairdresser's and it was a windy day?

It's 1: a crowd-control tactic, of sorts. Apparently Putbroek FC were plagued by pitch invasions by a herd of wild pigs that dug up the turf in search of worms. It seems pigs have a highly developed sense of smell, and as soon as they catch a whiff of human scent, they scamper.

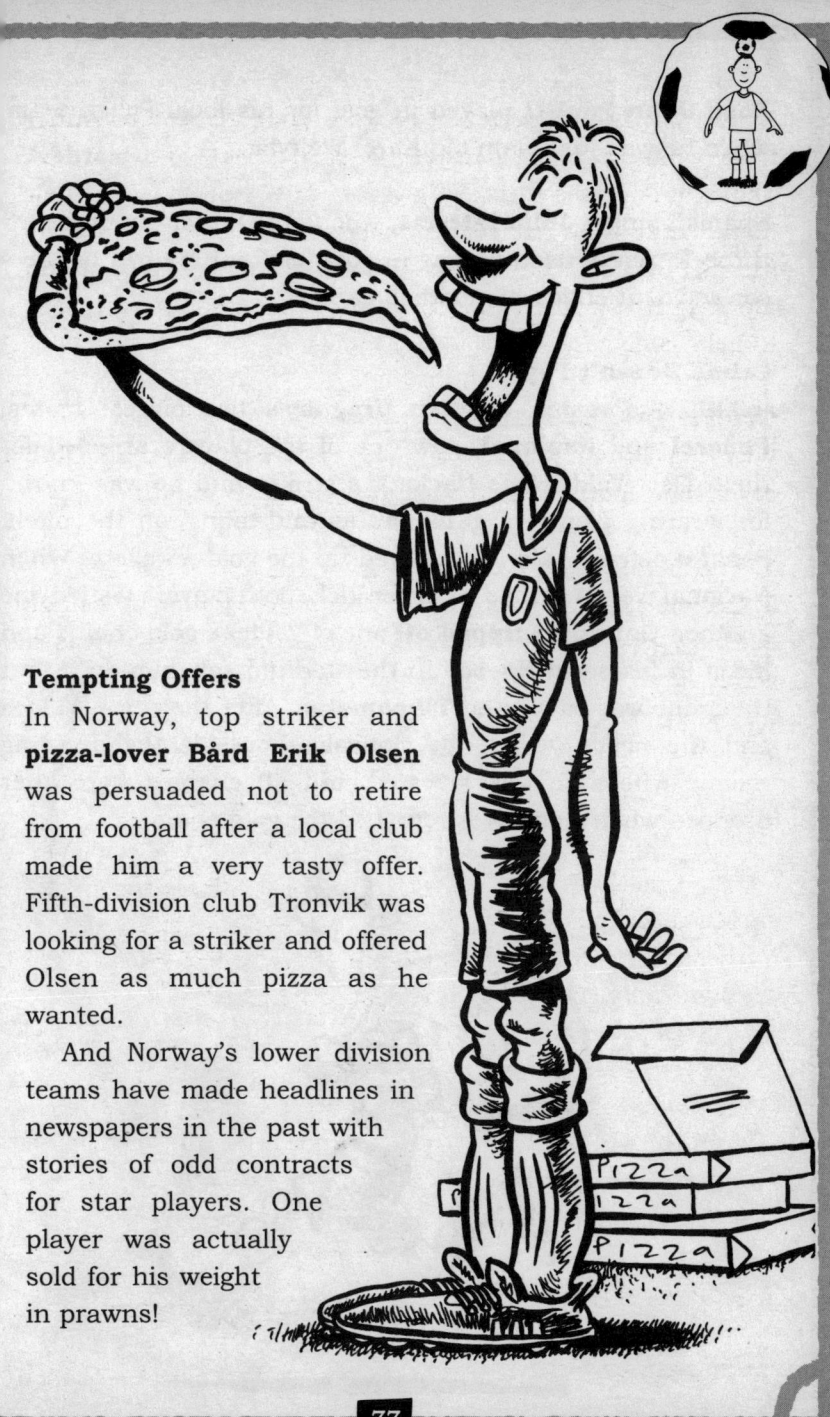

Tempting Offers

In Norway, top striker and **pizza-lover Bård Erik Olsen** was persuaded not to retire from football after a local club made him a very tasty offer. Fifth-division club Tronvik was looking for a striker and offered Olsen as much pizza as he wanted.

And Norway's lower division teams have made headlines in newspapers in the past with stories of odd contracts for star players. One player was actually sold for his weight in prawns!

Pope John Paul II played in goal for his local Polish team, when he was just plain old Karol Wojtyla.

Spanish singer **Julio Iglesias**, who is the father of pop heart-throb Enrique, used to play in goal for **Real Madrid** before a car accident ended his football career.

Crime Doesn't Pay

In 1991, a match between **Uruguay**'s two biggest teams, **Peñarol** and **Nacional**, saw one of the players arrested for theft. Dely Valdez was Nacional's striker and he was known for wearing plenty of **gold chains** and 'bling' on the pitch. Peñarol defender Goncalvez eyed up the gold jewellery. When Nacional were awarded a corner kick, both players jostled one another. Goncalvez **ripped off** one of Valdez's gold chains and hid it in his sock! Nobody in the stadium saw him do it, but the crime was caught on **TV cameras**. After the game, Valdez and the police waited for Goncalvez outside the dressing rooms, where he was arrested, but all charges were later dropped when Goncalvez returned the gold chain.

9. Wise Words

We'd be nowhere in football without players and managers shooting their mouths off or being generally thick! Here are some quotes to chuckle over about the Game of Two Halves.
However, one of them is totally made-up . . . Can you Find That Fib?

Managers' Gems

During the 1990s, **John Lambie** was manager of Scottish side Partick Thistle. When one of his players was concussed during a match, the team's trainer relayed the news to his boss that the poor player didn't know who he was. Lambie said, 'Tell him he's Pelé, and send him back on!'

Bill Shankly's Top Three
Legendary Liverpool manager Bill Shankly came up with some of the most quoted comments about the Glorious Game.

3. Shankly gave some words of advice to a youth player at Liverpool: 'The problem with you, son, is that your brains are all in your head.'

2. A football scout was trying to sell Bill Shankly a new player and proudly boasted to him, 'He has football in his blood.' 'You may be right,' Shankly replied, 'but it hasn't reached his legs yet!'

1. Then there was Shankly's classic quote: 'Some people believe football is a matter of life and death. I'm very disappointed with that attitude. I can assure you it is much, much more important than that.'

Sven-Göran Eriksson had quite a successful playing career with Swedish Second Division club KB Karlskoga and Degerfors, until an injury forced him to retire in 1975.

England manager **Sven-Göran Eriksson** showed an uncharacteristic show of emotion when asked what he disliked most about football. He said, 'It is not in my Scandinavian nature to dislike anything about football . . . apart from when you newspaper and TV reporters make up stories about my private life!' Then he burst into tears and turned away from the astonished TV interviewer.

Kevin Keegan's Top Five Memorable Quotes

Ex-England captain and top manager Kevin Keegan has had some unforgettable quotes:

5. 'Chile have three options – they could win or they could lose.'

4. 'I'll never play at Wembley again, unless I play at Wembley again.'

3. 'Bobby Robson must be thinking of throwing some fresh legs on.'

2. 'A tremendous strike which hit the defender full on the arm – and it nearly came off.'

1. 'They're the second-best team in the world, and there's no higher praise than that.'

Liverpool manager **Bob Paisley** once boasted:
'We've had the hard times too – one year we finished second.'

Here's a trio of quotes from ex-England supremo **Terry Venables**:
3. 'I felt a lump in my mouth as the ball went in.'
2. 'If you can't stand the heat in the dressing room, get out of the kitchen.'
1. 'If history is going to repeat itself, I should think we can expect the same thing again.'

Venison never really could get the hang of getting dressed before a match . . .

Football Commentators' Classics

'If that had gone in, it would have been a goal' – **David Coleman**

'I always used to put my right boot on first, and then obviously my right sock' – the wise words of ex-Liverpool player, and now commentator **Barry Venison**

'Zidane is not very happy, because he's suffering from the wind' – **Ron Atkinson**

'For those of you watching in black and white, Spurs are in the all-yellow strip' – **John Motson**

'With the very last kick of the game, Bobby McDonald scored with a header' – **Alan Parry**

Players' Classics
Newcastle legend **Alan Shearer** is very fond of his home town – and club – of Newcastle. He once said, 'I've never wanted to leave. I'm here for the rest of my life, and hopefully after that as well.'

Ex-England goalie **Peter Shilton** wasn't brilliant at keeping team spirits up when he said, 'You've got to believe that you're going to win, and I believe we'll win the World Cup until the final whistle blows and we're knocked out.'

Stan Collymore made things as clear as mud when he said, 'I faxed a transfer request to the club at the beginning of the week, but let me state that I don't want to leave Leicester.'

Roy Keane once snarled, 'I don't think some of the people who come to Old Trafford can spell football, never mind understand it.'

You wouldn't argue with **Stuart 'Psycho' Pearce**, even when he came out with a sentence like, 'I can see the carrot at the end of the tunnel.'

Explaining why he had leapt into the crowd and karate-kicked a Crystal Palace fan, Manchester United's moody French striker **Eric Cantona** baffled everyone by saying, 'When the seagulls follow the trawler, it's because they think sardines will be thrown into the sea.' Cantona's strange comment didn't help him – he was banned from playing football for nine months.

David Beckham's Top Three

3. 'Alex Ferguson is the best manager I've ever had at this level. Well, he's the only manager I've actually had at this level. But he's the best manager I've ever had.'

2. 'My parents have been there for me, ever since I was about seven.'

1. 'Some people think that I haven't got the brains to be that clever.'

'I couldn't settle in Italy – it was like living in a foreign country'
– ex-Liverpool and Wales international **Ian Rush**.

'Sometimes in football you have to score goals' Arsenal's
Thierry Henry feels it is necessary to state the obvious.

But the last word must remain with **Pelé**, who said,
'Football. It's the beautiful game.'

10. World Cup Stories

Just before the final whistle is blown, there's a chance for you to see if you can Find That Fib among this world-class selection of footballing facts, all cleverly connected with that most famous of tournaments – the World Cup.

England's World Cup Record
1930, 1934, 1938
England didn't enter the competition.

1950
In Brazil, England's first World Cup trip ended in misery after the United States beat them 1–0.

1954
In Switzerland, England bowed out at quarter-final stage, losing 4–2 to Uruguay.

1958

In Sweden, England's hopes were dashed with the 1–0 defeat by the then USSR in a Group Four play-off game.

1962

In Chile, England lost 3–1 in their quarter-final against Brazil.

1966

This was England's finest hour: as host nation England beat West Germany 4–2 in the final at Wembley.

1970

In Mexico, England lost 3–2 to West Germany in the quarter-finals.

1974, 1978

England failed to qualify. Boo-hoo!

1982

In Spain, England went out after draws against West Germany and the host nation.

1986

In Mexico, England were seen off in the quarter-finals by Argentina, as they lost 2–1 – thanks mainly to Diego Maradona's sneaky handball.

1990

In Italy, Paul 'Gazza' Gascoigne cried after England made it to the semi-finals, but lost on penalties against West Germany.

1994

England failed to qualify. Boo-hoo, again!

1998

In France, England made it to the second round, where Michael Owen scored a fantastic goal and David Beckham got sent off, leaving Argentina to win on penalties.

2002

In the Japan and Korea World Cup, England made it to the quarter-final, where they were beaten 2–1 by Brazil. Though Michael Owen had opened the scoring, Rivaldo equalized and pony-tailed goalie David 'Safe Hands'

Seaman made an uncharacteristic error when he failed to stop Ronaldinho's free kick.

2006
Win or lose, fill in that World Cup winning result here:

Handy World Cup Winners' Summary

South America leads the way, with nine World Cup wins. They're closely followed by Europe, with eight World Cup wins.

1. Brazil – 1958, 1962, 1970, 1994, 2002 (5 titles)
2. Germany – 1954, 1974, 1990 (3 titles)
   Italy – 1934, 1938, 1982 (3 titles)
3. Argentina – 1978, 1986 (2 titles)
   Uruguay – 1930, 1950 (2 titles)
4. England – 1966 (1 title)
   France – 1998 (1 title)

WORLD CUP 2006

OK, footie fans – here's a burst of world-class facts about the World Cup contenders for 2006!

GROUP A

Germany – This is the second time Germany has hosted the World Cup – the first was in 1974. All eyes this year will be on Berlin's massive Olympia stadium which has a capacity for 74,500 seats.

Costa Rica - was the first country in the world to get rid of its army. However, Los Ticos will try to play with military precision in their third World Cup.

Poland – Southampton's Kamil Kosowski is one of three Saints players in the national squad, along with striker Grzegorz Rasiak and goalie Batosz Bialkowski.

Ecuador – This country has one of the world's greatest concentrations of active volcanoes, but will Villa's Ulysses de la Cruz be hot stuff on the pitch?

GROUP B

England – will 2006 be England's finest World Cup performance since 1966? Fingers, toes and everything else crossed for the Three Lions!

Paraguay – in the last two World Cups, Paraguay have been knocked out by the eventual finalists . . . Can we make it three in a row?

Trinidad & Tobago – England midfielder Chris Birchall will be playing for the Soca Warriors. He qualified because his mother was born in the capital, Port of Spain.

Sweden – Swedish striker Zlatan Ibrahimovic is so skilful on the Juventus pitch, he has been called 'half ballerina, half gangster'.

GROUP C

Argentina – Chelsea's Argentinian forward Hernán Crespo is one of the world's most expensive players of all time. His combined transfer fee is a staggering £68,000,000 – so his World Cup performance should be worth watching!

Ivory Coast – will have 21-year-old Gunners defender Emmanuel Eboue playing for them.

Serbia & Montenegro – Portsmouth's Dejan Stefanovic will be playing. He has what sports writers call an 'educated left foot'.

Holland - If the Dutch players clear a ball by whacking it straight up in the air, you now know that it's called a vuurpijl, a word which means 'rocket'.

GROUP D

Mexico – Bolton Wanderers fans will no doubt stop to cheer on Jared Borgetti as he plays for Mexico.

Iran – three times champions of Asia, Iran are playing in their second World Cup tournament thanks to goals from veteran top scorer, 36 year-old Ali Dael.

Angola – When Angola last played Portugal in 2001, four Angolan players were sent off and the ref abandoned the game. This is Angola's sixth attempt to qualify for the World Cup.

Portugal – the national team reached their first major final at Euro 2004 where they lost out to Greece. In 1966, England beat them in the World Cup semi-final.

GROUP E

Italy – a research poll has shown that almost 40% of Italian fans following the sky-blue Azzuri at the World Cup 2006 will be women.

Ghana – the national team, known as the Black Stars, has won the African Cup of Nations four times. This is the country's debut World Cup appearance.

USA – Bobby Convey plays for Reading, but he'll need all his youthful skills to help USA through their games in this difficult 'Group of Death'.

Czech Republic – striker Milan Baros plays in the UK for Aston Villa, scoring for them just 10 minutes after his debut game against Blackburn in 2005.

GROUP F

Brazil –When players want to 'nutmeg' the ball, they yell 'drible da vaca', which literally means, 'the cow's dribble'. These World Cup champions are also the favourites for 2006.

Croatia – two players to watch out for are Dado Prso, who plays for Glasgow Rangers and Portsmouth's Ivica Mornar.

Australia – Josip Skoko may be a vital player in the national Oz side, but he has problems getting a first team place at his club – Wigan!

Japan – qualified in 2006 for its third consecutive World Cup, but will 'The Blues' be feeling the blues if they get knocked out early?

GROUP G

France – When the French want to describe the team at the bottom of the league, they call them 'lanterne rouge' which means 'red lantern'. It's unlikely that they will be at the bottom of the heap this year.

Switzerland – this is their seventh World Cup final qualification and skipper Johann Vogel hopes that a mix of young and experienced players will make a difference.

South Korea – the national team hopes rest with Man U's Park Ji Sung (also known as 'Hub Lub') and Spurs' young signing, Lee Young-Pyo.

Togo – Arsenal signing Emmanuel Sheyi Adebayor led his country to their first World Cup finals after top-scoring in the African zone.

GROUP H

Spain – captain Raúl, known as the Angel from Madrid, is the most-capped outfielder in Spanish football history. Each time he scores a goal, he kisses his wedding ring.

Ukraine – the first European team to qualify for the 2006 World Cup, they have high hopes for goals from AC Milan's Andriy Shevchenko, 2004's European Footballer of the Year.

Tunisia – reigning African champions Tunisia head for Germany in 2006 for a third consecutive World Cup appearance, which will be their fourth overall.

Saudi Arabia – nicknamed 'The Sons Of The Desert', their local fans know them as al-Sogour or al-Akhdar, which means 'The Green' as shown in their away strip...

Home Nations in the World Cup
Scotland have managed to qualify for eight World Cup finals, including every World Cup from 1974 to 1990. Sadly, though, they've never got beyond the first round.

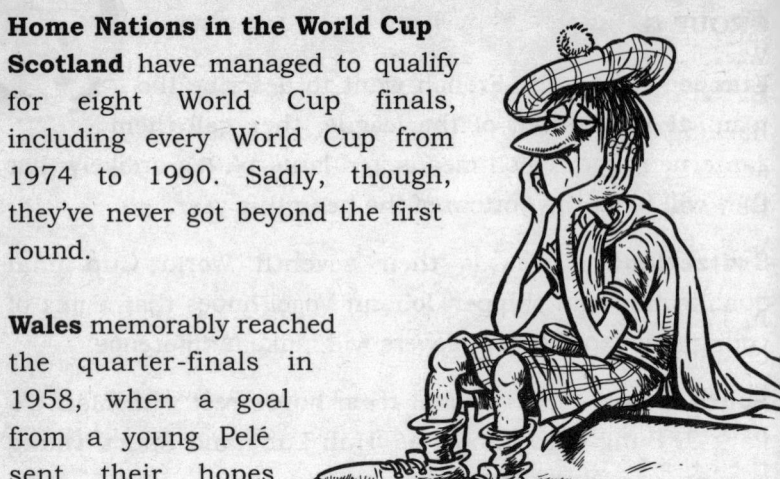

Wales memorably reached the quarter-finals in 1958, when a goal from a young Pelé sent their hopes crashing.

Northern Ireland have qualified for three World Cups, reaching the quarter-finals in 1958 and unforgettably beating host nation Spain in 1982, before going out in the second round.

The Republic of Ireland have qualified three times – in 1990, when they got to the quarter-finals, in 1994 and again in 2002.

World Cup Records
The **fastest goal** ever scored in a World Cup match was put in the back of the net by **Turkey's Hakan Sükür** after only 11 seconds against **South Korea** in 2002.

The **latest** World Cup goal was scored by England's **David Platt**, in their second-round game against **Belgium** in 1990. Platty slotted the ball in the net after 119 minutes.

France's **Lucian Laurent** scored the first ever World Cup goal against Mexico in 1930.

The record for the fastest sending-off during a World Cup match is held by **Uruguay's José Batista**. He got awarded the red card for cynically hacking down **Scotland's Gordon Strachan** after 56 seconds during the 1986 Mexico World Cup. Of course, Batista claimed he hadn't meant to do it, but the ref said, "No way, José!"

In **1934**, **Uruguay** refused to travel to Italy for the World Cup championships because they were annoyed so few European teams had bothered to attend the previous tournament. That makes Uruguay the only World Cup champs **not to defend** their title.

In the **1938** World Cup, held in France, brilliant Brazilian striker **Leonidas** scored a **hat-trick** against Poland. When he tried to play the second half **barefoot** – because he thought it would make him play even better – the referee ordered him to put his boots back on. Leonidas was in such a **strop** that Poland started scoring goals themselves.

Eventually, he pulled himself together and scored again. His four goals helped Brazil to win that game by 6 goals to 5 in extra time.

The only **brothers** to **play together** in an England World Cup team are **Bobby and Jack Charlton** in the **1966** World Cup...which England won.

Other famous football siblings, the Neville brothers, never achieved that same honour.

Gary Neville was part of Glenn Hoddle's 1998 England World Cup Squad. His brother Phil burst into tears when he heard he'd been left out of Hoddle's squad in favour of Paul Gascoigne.

Neither Neville made it to the 2002 World Cup Squad as Gary was injured and Phil wasn't picked.

In the **1970** World Cup, England manager **Sir Alf Ramsey** left nothing to chance when it came to protecting his defending champions. Sir Alf thought Mexican food would upset the stomachs of his boys, so guess what he took on tour:

a) 63 kg of burgers, 180 kg of bangers, 136 kg of fish and 10 cases of tomato ketchup
b) A bucket for each player
c) A crate of Alka-Seltzer

Answer (a). After all that effort it was a shame that goalie Gordon Banks missed the quarter-final against Germany because of...tummy trouble!

The only World Cup record won by tiny **Togo** in West Africa is having appeared in all the World Cup contests – apart from 2002, when they didn't qualify. In every contest, however, they've finished bottom of their group at the opening stage. That means they've been **knocked out** a staggering **17** times. Yet every four years, they've still come back for more.

After what's been called a 'smartball' experiment at FIFA's Under-17 World Championship, the 2006 World Cup will be the first to use space-age technology to confirm a goal. A **microchip** placed in the ball will send a signal to the referee once that ball crosses the goal line.

World Cup Trophy Facts

The **Jules Rimet Cup** is the official name of the original World Cup, named after FIFA's most famous president – the man who came up with the idea in the first place. It was permanently held by Brazil after their third World Cup win in Mexico City in 1970.

Since Brazil took ownership of the Jules Rimet Cup, FIFA have created a new trophy, the **FIFA World Cup**, which features the famous design of two players holding up the earth. The base has enough room for the names of the winning teams right up until 2038.

Nowadays, the winning World Cup team has the trophy for just **four years** and gets to keep a **gold-plated replica**.

The World Cup trophy was first **stolen** while on display in March **1966**, just three months before the tournament was due to start in London. A **dog** called **Pickles** found it wrapped in newspaper and stuffed under a hedge. His owner got £3,000 reward for the find, plus a year's free supply of dog food for clever old Pickles!

The World Cup was **stolen once again** in **1983**, when two men entered the Brazilian Soccer Federation building, tied up the guard and snatched the cup from its armour-plated, bullet-proof case. Despite a reward being offered of more than $1,050, the trophy was **never recovered**. Made from 1.8 kilograms of gold, it was probably **melted** down. The Brazilian Football Federation replaced it with their own replica.

During **World War II**, the cup was put in a **shoebox** by Dr Ottorino Barassi, the Italian FIFA vice-president. He then hid it under his bed so that the **Nazis** wouldn't steal it.

Football Voodoo

The **Australian** football team the **Socceroos** have traditionally considered Australian football to be **cursed** since trying to win a place in the Mexico World Cup of 1970. The team enlisted the help of a Mozambican **witch doctor** to put a **curse** on their rivals from Zimbabwe (then known as Rhodesia). The Socceroos won 3–1, but couldn't pay the voodoo man his moolah – not surprisingly as the witch doc had demanded $100,000! The not-so-good doctor was so angry when they refused to pay that he put a curse on the Aussie team. The Socceroos' appearance in the 2006 World Cup helped convince fans down under that the spell had finally lifted. However, there was still a certain voodoo in the fact that their group – Group F – was led by those mighty World Cup champions Brazil.

Top Three World Cup Scorers (up until the 2006 World Cup)

1. 14 goals – Gerd Muller (Germany)
2. 13 goals – Just Fontaine (France)
3. 12 goals – Pelé and Ronaldo (Brazil)

The winner of the most goals scored in the World Cup tournament always receives the Golden Boot Award...

World Cup Mascots

The official 2006 World Cup mascot is a lion called Goleo VI. He has a special friend, however – a talking football called Pille. They're made by the Jim Henson Company – the company behind the Muppets.

Three Other World Cup Mascots You Won't Remember

1. World Cup Willie, England's footballing lion from the World Cup glory year of 1966. (Willie was the World Cup's first mascot – and some would say the best!)
2. Footix the cartoon cockerel from France, 1998
3. Striker, the ball-juggling hound-dog from the USA, 1994.

England's Chances in the 2006 World Cup

Before their Group B draw against England, Sweden and Paraguay, **Trinidad & Tobago** had never played in a World Cup. The Soca Warriors were **captained** by ex-Man U and Blackburn striker **Dwight Yorke**. He came out of international retirement to lead his team which was largely made up of players from England's lower leagues like Falkirk, Port Vale and Crewe.

Paraguay have only played England twice before. In the **1986** World Cup, they were beaten 3–0, and in a **2002** friendly, England beat them 4–0. Paraguay's manager – Anibil Ruiz – was quoted in 2005 as saying that his favourite England players were Paul Scholes (who is now retired) and Roy Keane (who is Irish).

Sweden were the team that coach Sven-Göran Eriksson anticipated would be the **biggest threat** to England – thanks largely to Henrik Larsson and Zlatan Ibrahimovic. Sven's rival coach and fellow Swede – Lars Lagerback – reckoned that his deadly duo '…are at the same level as Michael Owen and Wayne Rooney.' Sweden went into the 2006 World Cup knowing that they haven't been beaten by England since 1968.

11. Find That Fib...

Chapter 1. Football History

If you believed that nonsense about Vikings using wooden footballs to play games in honour of their sun god, then I'm afraid you got fooled!

If you *didn't* believe it, then well done – you Found That Fib!

However, it is true that in France people used to play a version of football called *La Soule*, which was a rough translation of their word for 'sun'. In this game, the ball was thrown high into the air to make it look just like the sun, and games were played on Sundays until sunset.

Chapter 2. Football Legends

If you didn't believe that nonsense about Mark Hughes being a trainee electrician and kicking a ball that damaged a floodlight, then well done – you Found That Fib! Although, it is a fact that Mark Hughes actually joined Man U after leaving school in 1980 – and his first name is actually Leslie . . . but no one ever calls him that! They generally still call him 'Sparky' cos it rhymes with Mark.

Chapter 3. Just for the Record

If you didn't believe that nonsense about two Welsh schoolgirls holding the record for heading a football between themselves, then well done! You Found That Fib!

However, Kosovo's Agim Agushi and his equally skilled mate Bujar Ajeti actually do hold the record for heading a football between one another. Agim and Bujar headed it back and forth 11,111 times in just under four hours on 9 November 2003 in Starnberg, Germany.

Chapter 4. Freaky Injuries

If you didn't believe that silly story about Thierry Henry getting tangled with a sweeping brush during a game, then congratulations – you Found That Fib!

Although it is totally true that a few years ago Henry was celebrating a goal for Arsenal against Chelsea and, unfortunately, hit himself in the face with the corner flag, which meant a trip to the treatment room.

Chapter 5. Oi, Ref!

If you didn't believe the story about clubs named Totnes Academicals and Whitchurch Rangers, and a ref booking 37 insult-shouting fans, then . . . you Found That Fib!

Although it is a fact that Chorley player Stuart Tulloch was actually booked by a referee for excessively celebrating . . . while sitting on the bench! Stuart was wearing a T-shirt not his footy kit – and he wasn't even part of his team's squad for that day!

Chapter 6. Footy Fans

If you didn't believe that silly tale that Ludwig van Beethoven wrote a football chant, then let's sing your praises – you Found That Fib!

However, it is believed that one of the earliest football chants was written by classical composer Sir Edward Elgar (a fan of Wolverhampton Wanderers). Elgar set the words 'He banged the leather for goal!' to music in praise of Wolves player Billy Malpas. It is not thought that his chant was widely used on the terraces.

Chapter 7. Home Ground

Congratulations if you didn't believe that nonsense about Sir Sean Connery, Billy Connolly and Franz Ferdinand dressing up as Partick Thistle mascot, Pee Tee the Toucan. You Found That Fib.

The actual man dancing around inside the Pee Tee costume is Chester Studzinski, who lives in Glasgow. He claims that the original mascot for Partick Thistle was a thistle. However, too many people thought it actually looked like a turnip. That's why the club changed their mascot to a more easily recognizable toucan.

Chapter 8. Strange but True

If you didn't believe that story about Burnley playing in huge green platform boots with 7.5cm heels during the 1970s, then congratulations – you Found That Fib!

However, it is really true that Burnley wore a green football strip until 1911, when they were persuaded it was unlucky and changed colours . . .

Chapter 9. Wise Words

If you thought that quote from Sven-Göran Eriksson was totally made up, then congratulations . . . you Found That Fib!

However, when asked about an outburst from David Beckham, Sven did once reply, 'David should think that talking is silver, but being quiet is golden.'

Chapter 10. World Cup Stories

If you believed that nonsense about Togo having played in all the World Cup tournaments, then you're no champ at Finding the Fib! 2006 was Togo's debut at the World Cup, thanks to Emmanuel Sheyi Adebayor's 11 goals in qualifying games. Brazil is the only country to have played in all of the World Cup tournaments since the event started.